Heinrich

WOHLFAHRT

EASY FOUR HAND PIECES FOR CHILDREN

Opus 87

One Piano Four Hands

K 04039

The Musical Children's Friend

Secondo.

HEINRICH WOHLFAHRT. Op. 87.

The Musical Children's Friend.

Primo.

Not too fast. *Non troppo presto.*

HEINRICH WOHLFAHRT. Op. **87**.

Slowly. *Lento.*

4

Briskly. *Vivace.*　　　　　　　　Secondo.

Quietly. *Tranquillo.*

Briskly. *Vivace.*

3.

Quietly. *Tranquillo.*

4.

Secondo.

5.

Lively. *Allegretto.*

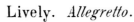

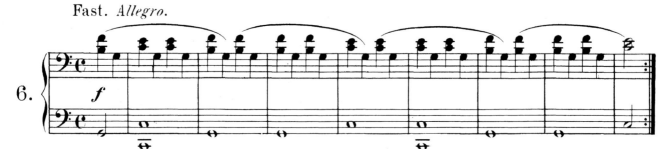

6.

Fast. *Allegro.*

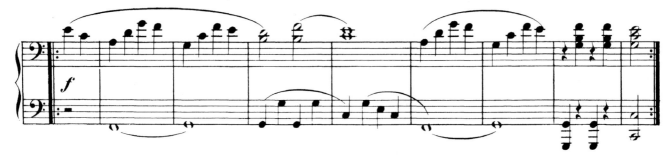

Lively. *Allegretto.*

5.

Fast. *Allegro.*

6.

Secondo.

Secondo.

With animation. *Con moto*.

10.

Not too fast. *Non troppo presto*.

11.

Secondo.

Moderately fast. *Moderato.*

Leisurely. *Comodo.*

Quietly. *Tranquillo.*

14.

Fast. *Allegro.*

15.

Moderately. *Moderato.*

16.

Secondo.

Secondo.

23.

Quietly. *Tranquillo.*

24.

With animation. *Con moto.*

25.

Not too fast. *Non troppo presto.*

Primo.

Secondo.

Primo.

26. Moderately. *Moderato.*

27. Slowly. *Adagio.*

Fine.

28. Briskly. *Vivace.*

D.C. al Fine.

Secondo.

Quietly. *Tranquillo.* **Secondo.**

Secondo.

35.

Very fast. *Presto.*

36.

Slowly. *Adagio.*

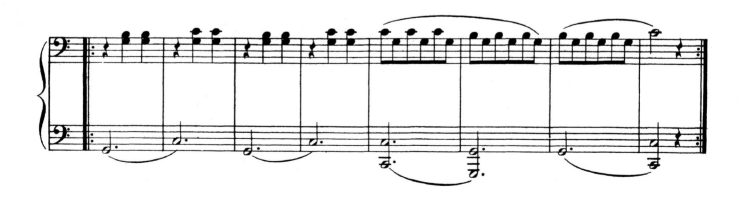

Primo.

Secondo.

Very fast. *Presto.*

Waltz.

Secondo.

Secondo.

Secondo.

Galop.

46.

Galop.

Secondo.

Secondo.